Writing: One Day at a Time

Exercises for young writers

By Liz Bass

Pieces of Learning

Cover by John Steele
© 2001 Pieces of Learning

www.piecesoflearning.com
CLC0260
ISBN 1-880505-97-5
Printed in the U.S.A.

A Sequential Approach to Writing Success

This book says **YES! to creativity, CERTAINLY! to flights of fancy**, and **OF COURSE! to good powers of observation.** Who needs this book? The answer is simple. Every student who is weary of humdrum writing assignments! It is a tonic for reluctant writers and, at the same time, a rejuvenation for the enthusiastic and gifted student.

Writing: one day at a time is designed to bring out the best in all students, regardless of where they are on the ladder of writing success. There are spelling exercises, grammar nudges, and vocabulary-building assignments.
There are a year's worth - 201 - opportunities to write stories, poems, essays, thank-you letters, paragraphs, and sentences. Included in **Writing: one day at a time** are prompts (Exercises) for **narratives** (stories with details, a beginning, middle and end); **expository writing** (instructional, informational explanation with examples); **persuasive writing** (persuasion with examples and details) and **descriptive writing.**
Research work is included. These Exercises can be assigned as **expository essays.**
Some of the exercises in the book are related to leadership; others to attitude. Some are related to the content areas: students are asked to locate Tierra del Fuego and Kosovo. They are asked to use their imaginations to describe someone whose name is "Rainey Knight."
Students are called upon to write stories based on nine words and other "story" Excerises can be selected as **narrative assignments;** their powers of observation are called upon to describe their eye-witness accounts of a car accident in a **descriptive essay.**
Opinion pieces are requested about topics such as "Why is forgiveness so difficult for most people?" or "How is road rage related to respect?"These can be assigned as **persuasive/point of view essays.**
If you want to nurture lively writing in your classes, this is the book for you. The exercises are fun to do, so the students will go at them with gusto. They will find in the exercises a host of new connections between themselves and the world around them.
When all the exercises are completed, students will have created for themselves a journal they will want to save for the future.

Writing: one day at a time   Exercises for Young Writers

If you avoid writing because you think you're not any good at it, here's a little Exercise Journal that may hold promise for you.

Can it put a stop to the **angst** you experience whenever the subject of writing comes up?

Can it help you become a self-respecting writer? Good questions.

By the way, feel free to look up **angst** or any other word you're not sure about. It is a painless thing to do, and it has a payoff. You'll learn the definition of the word, and, in turn, you will know more about the meaning of any sentence which **houses** the word.

Houses it? Sure, why not? You could say includes it, or **contains** it, or a lot of other things. I like **houses**, so that's why I'm using it. It says what I mean and at the same time, pulls up an unexpected image that may catch a reader's attention.

Speaking of readers, just remember that they're **rooting** for you. They want to read about interesting things written in interesting ways, and they're always hoping that writers can deliver. If they hoped otherwise, it would be **curtains** for writers. Readers would leave all the written material that comes their way on hall table trash piles.

In the best of all worlds, readers root for writers and writers root for readers. Each shows respect for the other. **Keep that idea in mind as you work through this book.** All right. Enough said. Let's see what we can do about this *writing thing*. Let's pump some iron!

Exercise 1:

Choose any five letters in the alphabet. For each letter you choose, write a sentence in which every word begins with that letter. For example, if you choose the letter "a" your sentence might read:

Alfred always ate alone.

1. _____

2. _____

3. _____

4. _____

5. _____

Have more? Go for it!

_____

_____

Exercise 2:

Write a sentence in which the first word is *We*.

We _____

Write a sentence in which the last word is *yesterday*.

_____ yesterday.

Write a sentence in which the fourth word is *time*.

_____ time _____

Exercise 3:

Define these words:

they're _____   you're _____

who's _____   their _____

its _____   whose _____

there _____   it's _____

whom_____

Exercise 4:

Find at least two meanings for each of the following <u>suffixes</u>:

-ese _____   _____

-logy _____   _____

-ism _____   _____

-er   _____   _____

-ness _____   _____

Other meanings:

Exercise 5:

Beginnings

Give the principal meaning of each of the following <u>prefixes</u>:

bi- _____   di- _____

in- _____   mis- _____   de- _____

ex- _____   re- _____   pre- _____

Exercise 6:

Give five examples of *colloquial* words or phrases. Define what each one means.

5. _____

_____

4. _____

_____

3. _____

_____

2. _____

_____

1. _____

_____

Exercise 7:

Name the eight parts of speech.

1. _____   2. _____   3. _____

4. _____   5. _____   6. _____

7. _____   8. _____

Exercise 8:

What does each of the following words mean when used as a noun?
How about when used as a verb?

	Noun		Verb
slug			
quibble			
boil			
sentence			
slur			
salt			
wonder			
pen			
act			

Exercise 9:

Write a sentence using *salt* as a noun. Then write another one using *salt* as a verb.

Exercise 10:

What do these words mean?

feat _____

anecdote _____

illuminated _____

affect _____

effect _____

affliction _____

email _____

fax _____

indiscriminately _____

Exercise 11:

What do <u>nouns</u> describe? _____

Name five proper nouns and five common nouns. Remember to capitalize the proper nouns!

<u>Proper</u>   <u>common</u>

Exercise 12:

What do <u>verbs</u> describe? _____

List five verbs in both
their past and present tense forms.

<u>Present tense</u>   **<u>Past tense</u>**

Exercise 13

Write a sentence in which the fifth word is *feat*.

_____feat_____

_____

Write a sentence which contains the terms *fax* and *email*.

_____

Write a sentence which correctly uses the word *affect*.

_____

Exercise 14:

Explain the function of <u>pronouns.</u>

Pronouns _____ /\ the /\ of _____

List six pronouns.

1.   4.

2.   5

3.   6.

Exercise 15:

What do these words mean? Draw a symbol for each.

quickness	cherish
squander	ingredients

Exercise 16:

List seven <u>adjectives</u> and then use each in a separate sentence.

1.
2.
3.
4.
5.
6.
7.

Exercise 17:

What functions do <u>adverbs</u> have in sentences?
List eight. Then use each in sentences.   My Sentence(s):

1. _____   2. _____

3. _____   4. _____

5. _____   6. _____

7. _____   8. _____

Exercise 18:

What is the definition of a _sentence_?

_____

What is a _run-on_ sentence?

_____

What is a _predicate_?

_____

 What _ingredients_ must every sentence have?

_____

Exercise 19:

Learn to spell the following words. Take a test when you are ready. Use the _honor system_ or find a teacher or _proctor_ who is willing to help.

stamina   extraneous

attitude   metaphor

ignore   descriptive

Exercise 20:

Write a sentence that uses the words _all right_. Then write another sentence using the words _all wrong_.

Exercise 21:

What is an <u>interjection</u>?

Write five sentences that have interjections in them.

1.

2.

3.

4.

5.

Exercise 22:

Give five examples of <u>exclamations</u>.

1.

2.

3.

4.

5.

Exercise 23:

Name three types of sentences and write an example of each.

1. _____

2. _____

3. _____

Exercise 24:

List five words that end in *-ism.*

List five words that end in *-ness.*

List five words that end in *-er.*

Exercise 25:

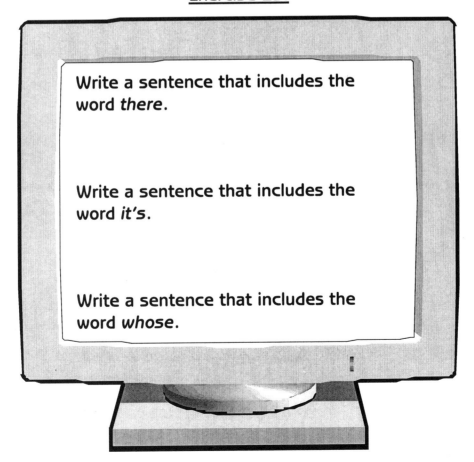

Write a sentence that includes the word *there.*

Write a sentence that includes the word *it's.*

Write a sentence that includes the word *whose.*

Exercise 26:

Write a sentence in which the first word is *Their*.

Their _____

_____

Write a sentence in which the first word is *You're*.

You're _____

_____

Write a sentence in which the first word is *Who's*.

Who's _____

_____

Exercise 27:

What do these words mean?

optimist

vignette

percussion

artistic

misanthrope

athletic

Exercise 28:

What do people mean when they say "*no problem*?" What does "*no way*" mean? If a person makes a statement and then follows it immediately with the word "*not*," what's the message?

Exercise 29:

What does *RSVP* stand for? _____

What do the following abbreviations stand for?

S _ _ _ _ _

I _ _ _ _ _

D _ _ _ _

S _ _ _ _ _ _ _

V _ _ _

I _ _ _ _ _ _ _ _

P _ _ _ _ _

A _____

I _____

D _____

S _____

Exercise 30:

What do these words mean?

biology - *the study of* _____

theology - *the study of* _____

forgiveness -

metaphor -

tolerance -

concentrate -

workaholic -

genuine -

Exercise 31:

When a person experiences <u>*angst*</u>, what feelings does he or she typically have? Draw your interpretation of *angst*.

Exercise 32:

Of what value are <u>*metaphors*</u> in speaking and writing?

Do they <u>*muddy the waters*</u> or do they make ideas easier to understand? Explain.

Exercise 33:

Respond to the idea in the following paragraph:

"Writing is not all that popular these days because
people like faster means of communication.
We want to know what's happening immediately. We _fax_. We _email_.
We like _quickness_. We _cherish_ time. We hate to _squander_ it."

_____

_____

_____

_____

_____

_____

Exercise 34:

What is your opinion of this idea?

"When you ignore people who are mean to you,
they will eventually ignore you too."

Exercise 35:

Respond to these questions:

How important is <u>attitude</u> in life?
What can you tell about a person's *attitude* by the way he or she dresses?
Can people *conceal* their *attitudes*?
How can language *reveal* a person's *attitude*?

Exercise 36:

Write a sentence that uses the word _act_ as a noun.

_____

Write a sentence that uses the word _act_ as a verb.

_____

Write a sentence that uses the word _effect_.

_____

Write a sentence that uses the word _illuminated_.

_____

Write a sentence that uses the word _quibble_ as a verb.

_____

Write a sentence that uses the word _wonder_ as a noun.

_____

Exercise 37:

What do these terms mean? What do they look like?

muddy the waters   honor system

big picture   corporal punishment

road rage   personal best

<u>Exercise 38</u>:

Write a sentence that includes the word <u>*stamina*</u>.

_____

Write a sentence that includes the word <u>*grace*</u>.

_____

Write a sentence that includes the word <u>*extraneous*</u>.

_____

<u>Exercise 39</u>:

abcdefghijklmnopqrstuvwxyz

Choose another five letters in the alphabet. For each letter you choose, write a sentence in which every word begins with that letter. For example, if you choose the letter "f" your sentence might read:

Frank found fourteen financial forms.

1.

2.

3.

4.

5.

Exercise 40:

What do these words mean? Give examples of each.

synonym _____

_____

. _____

antonym _____

_____

_____

homonym _____

_____

_____

homily _____

_____

_____

adage _____

_____

_____

wisecrack _____

_____

_____

Exercise 41:

Make a list of ten things you did last Sunday.

Exercise 42:

Make a list of ten things you expect to do next week.

Exercise 43:

Make a list of six advantages of being very rich.

$ $

$ $

$ $

Exercise 44:

Make a list of ten things which bore you.

Exercise 45:

Make a list of fifteen things that are beautiful.

1.   2.   3

4.   5.   6.

7.   8.   9.

10.   11.   12

13.   14.   15.

Exercise 46:

Make a list of everything that was in your refrigerator last night.

Exercise 47:

Make a list of your closest friends and then another one of people you think may be enemies. Are the lists the same length?

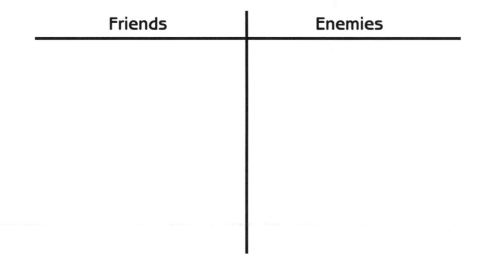

Friends	Enemies

Exercise 48:

Make a list of places that you think would make good vacation spots.

U.S.A.

Exercise 49:

Make a list of things you have done well over the past year.

Exercise 50:

Make a list of your relatives.

Exercise 51:

Make a list of the places you go during a normal week in your life.

Exercise 52:

Make a list of ingredients that you would use to make spaghetti.

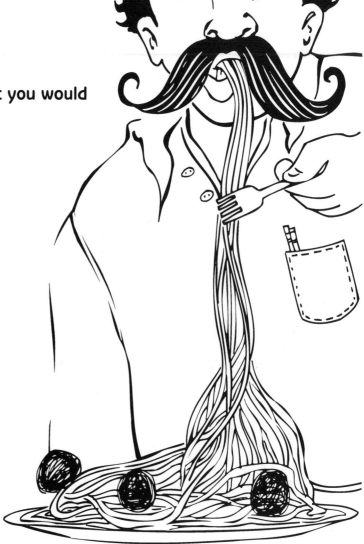

Exercise 53:

Make a list of landmarks a person can see while visiting the state in which you live.

Exercise 54:

Make a list of character traits you admire in people.

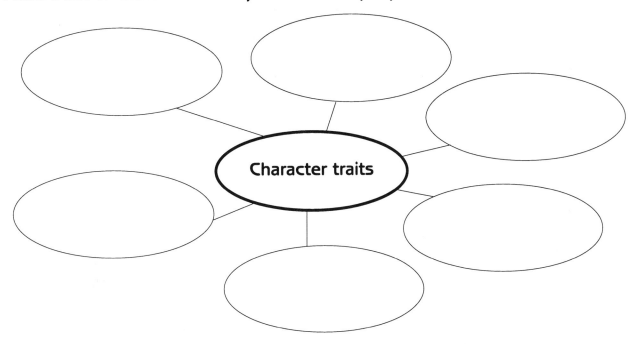

Exercise 55:

Make a list of your good points.

Exercise 56:

When writers or speakers use the expression "*curtains*," they may mean that something is finished. What's the connection between an end to something and the expression *curtains*? If a writer uses the word *curtains* to express this meaning, is he or she describing something good or not-so-good?

Exercise 57:

What do these expressions mean? When would you use the expression?

body language _____

_____

c'est la vie _____

_____

the cat's pajamas _____

_____

missed the boat _____

_____

birth order _____

_____

coup d'etat _____

_____

salad days _____

_____

bull market _____

_____

halcyon days _____

_____

the Midas touch _____

_____

Exercise 58:

Write four sentences which say essentially what this one does:

"It seemed that his aunt often yelled at him for no reason."

1.

2.

3.

4.

Exercise 59:

Define these words:

abstract

vague

ephemeral

aphorism

simile

analogy

Exercise 60:

Go to a place that you think might be quiet for about five minutes. Bring a pencil and paper. *Concentrate* on sounds in the background you might otherwise ignore. Identify the source of the sounds you hear. Write those sources down in list form.

Exercise 61:

 Describe your kitchen.

Exercise 62:

 Explain how to brew a pot of coffee.

Exercise 63:

 Explain how to mail a letter. Don't forget the stamp!

Exercise 64:

Describe two family members.

Describe two friends.

Exercise 65:

Explain how to get from your home to the capitol of your State. Use route numbers.

Exercise 66:

Explain the procedure you prefer for making macaroni and cheese.

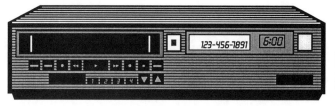

Exercise 67:

Explain how to program a VCR to show the correct time.

Exercise 68:

Explain how to gain access to the Internet.

Exercise 69:

Explain how to drive a car with an automatic clutch.

Exercise 70:

Explain the process for learning how to type.

Exercise 71:

Explain the process for voting in a general election.

Exercise 72:

Describe the characters and action in your favorite television show.

Exercise 73:   In exactly one hundred words, describe yourself. (Try 10 words per line!)

_____

_____

_____

_____

_____

_____

_____

_____

_____

Exercise 74:

Find a person who does not mind being observed for five minutes. Watch what the person does for that amount of time. The person could be a teacher, friend, or relative. You are the reporter at the scene. Write down everything you notice.

Exercise 75:

Write a response to this paragraph:

We have *a nagging sensation* that something is missing in our motor-driven society. In our most *illuminated moments,* we think it may be wisdom. *Somewhere deep inside,* we know that all of our modern gadgets have not made us smarter about living in harmony with each other and the natural environment.

Exercise 76:

Write at least two synonyms for each of the following words:

meat _____   _____

sanitary _____   _____

valid _____   _____

stupid _____   _____

stagnant _____   _____

successful _____   _____

Exercise 77:

Write four sentences which say essentially what this one does:

"He was a successful man, greatly admired by all."

Exercise 78:

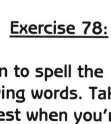

Learn to spell the
following words. Take a
test when you're
ready.

ridicule   praise
derision
commendation
criticism   respect

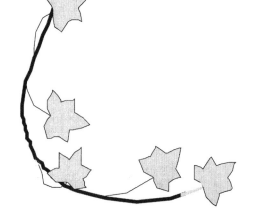

Exercise 79:

What does <u>courage</u> mean? Give examples.

Exercise 80:

Develop paragraphs from each of the following topic sentences.

1.   *Illumination takes many forms.*

2.   *She wanted to affect the outcome.*

3.   *Her voice produced an interesting effect on the crowd.*

4.   *"It's curtains for this relationship," she said with a grin.*

Exercise 81:

Write a paragraph using each of the following adjectives at least once. Use any other words you wish to connect them into a whole idea.

blue	light	cuddly	aromatic
vivid	rancid	hopeful	delicious

_____

_____

_____

_____

Exercise 82:

List the names of four television shows that were important to you as a child. List as many characters from the shows as you can recall.

1.

2.

3.

4.

Exercise 83:

What do these terms mean?

1. subject-verb agreement

2. prepositional phrase

3. conscientious objector

Exercise 84:

Write five sentences. Use a different adjective in each sentence:

beautiful   cunning   helpless   tangy   svelte

1.

2.

3.

4.

5.

Exercise 85:

What do these words mean?

obfuscate   *anecdote*

protruding   *ragamuffin*

Exercise 86

What is the difference between *then* and *than*?

Write a sentence using <u>then</u>. Write another sentence using <u>than</u>.

Exercise 87:

Write five sentences that use forms of the word _root_.

1.

2.

3.

4.

5.

Write sentences that show several ways to use the word.

Exercise 88:

Write a paragraph in the book that explains this statement:

"In the best of all worlds, readers root for writers and writers root for readers."

Exercise 89:

What does _shoplifting_ mean?

How about _edit_?

What is an _independent_ _clause_?

What is a _phrase_?

What is a _retraction_?

Exercise 90:

What does _empowerment_ mean?

Relate some _anecdotes_.

Exercise 91:

Name the five senses. Write an outline for an essay that describes the function of each. This is the topic sentence for the first paragraph:

Humans rely on their senses to gather information about their environment.

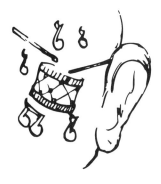

_____

_____

_____

_____

_____

Exercise 92:

Make a list of nine nouns. Make two of them proper nouns and seven of them common nouns. To save time, you can use the list below:

Martin   Mayflower   paper
    mother   thermometer   teacher
        school   flag   quiz

Exercise 93:

Write a paragraph using each of the nouns in <u>Exercise 92</u> at least once (or more if you want). You may use other words that are not on the list to connect the nouns into a whole idea. Here's an example:

Mrs. Sims, the mother of <u>*Martin Mayflower*</u>, *came to Martin's school to talk to his* <u>*teacher*</u> *about a* <u>*quiz*</u> *that* <u>*Martin*</u> failed. She also wanted to discuss something that she read in the paper about a broken <u>*thermometer*</u> in the gym and a tattered <u>*flag*</u> in the cafeteria.

Exercise 94:

Write a *vignette* that includes the following characters and words:

A Grammarian   A Masked Woman

    lemonade   communicators

       statues   sector

Use any other words you would like in order to connect them into a whole idea.

Exercise 95:

Write a *vignette* which includes each of the italicized words. Use any other words you need to connect everything together.

clumsy   *flying*   *sent*   *clown*   *bent*

empty   *sitting*   *alarm*   *room*

Exercise 96:

Write two paragraphs. In the first, praise yourself. In the second, criticize yourself.

Exercise 97:

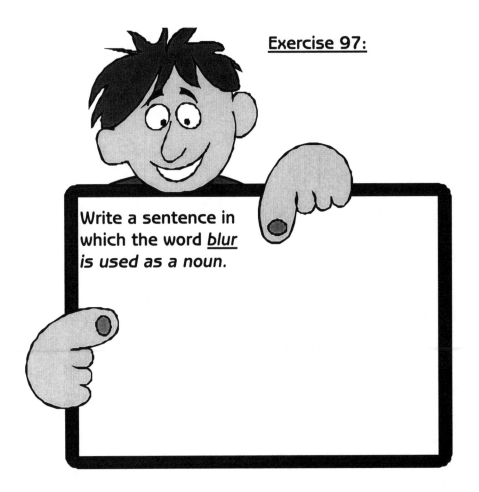

Write a sentence in which the word *blur* is used as a noun.

Exercise 98:

Write at least one paragraph about why pronouns are useful. Write another paragraph about why they often *blur* understanding.

Exercise 99:

Write a sentence in which the fifth word is _purse_.

Write a sentence containing three proper nouns.

Write a sentence containing two correctly positioned commas.

Write a sentence in which the first word is _Moving_.

Write a sentence which contains an action verb.

Exercise 100:

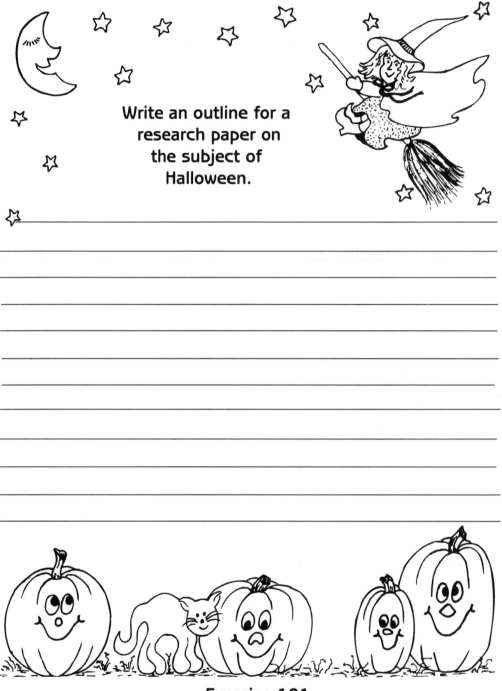

Write an outline for a research paper on the subject of Halloween.

_____

_____

_____

_____

_____

_____

_____

_____

_____

_____

_____

Exercise 101:

Research *Tierra Del Fuego*. Take notes. Then use your notes to construct an outline from which an essay can be based.

Exercise 102:

Develop paragraphs from the following topic sentences:

1. *He looked into her eyes.*

2. *There was no sound in the house.*

3. *Today is my birthday.*

4. *I knew the animal was dying.*

5. *What was the problem between them?*

6. *Her attitude said it all.*

Exercise 103:

Make a list of ten people you consider to be *heroes*.

1.   6.

2.   7.

3.   8.

4.   9.

5.   10.

Choose one person from your list and write about his or her heroic qualities.

Exercise 104:

Write a brief description of what you think people with the following names might look and act like:

Huxley Snivel   August Simper   Stanley Manley

Paul Crater   Starbright Perkins

Herbert Crazylegs

Blanche White

Rainey Knight

Exercise 105:

You have witnessed an accident at a four-way stop near your home. There were four cars involved. Two of them ran stop signs. Describe what you saw.

Exercise 106:

You are leaving on a vacation and have asked a neighbor to look after your place. Write a detailed explanation of what you want your neighbor to do.

Exercise 107:

Your Aunt Martha sent you a sweater she knitted herself. Write a *thank you note* to her.

Dear Aunt Martha,

Exercise 108:

Learn to spell the following words. Take a test when you are ready:

definition   inhibitions   paragraph   opportunity
advice   minority

Exercise 109:

You have seen a terrible commercial on television. Write to the station you were watching and complain.

Exercise 110:

You have just discovered that you are adopted. You have been given the address of your biological mother. Write a letter to her.

Exercise 111: A downtown park has been named after you in appreciation of all you have done for your town. Write the speech you will give at the dedication ceremony.

Exercise 112:

You have received a letter from a friend who tells you he has developed a shoplifting habit. Write back to your friend. Tell him what you think of this. Offer some advice.

Exercise 113:

Imagine that you are about eight months old. Write how you would feel about being left alone in the back yard.

Exercise 114:

You are thirty years old and afraid of the dark. Trace the history of your fear.

Exercise 115:

You have just entered your seven-year-old child in a new school. You receive a notice from the school asking permission to administer *corporal punishment* to your child when the Principal thinks it necessary. The note lists several of the school's methods of punishment, including slapping, paddles, and banishment to a dark room. Write a letter to the school telling of your wishes in this matter.

Exercise 116:

The telephone company sent you an incorrect bill for a $75.00 long distance call. You called the phone company twice to complain, but nothing has been done. The company has now threatened to shut off your service. Write a letter to the company about this situation.

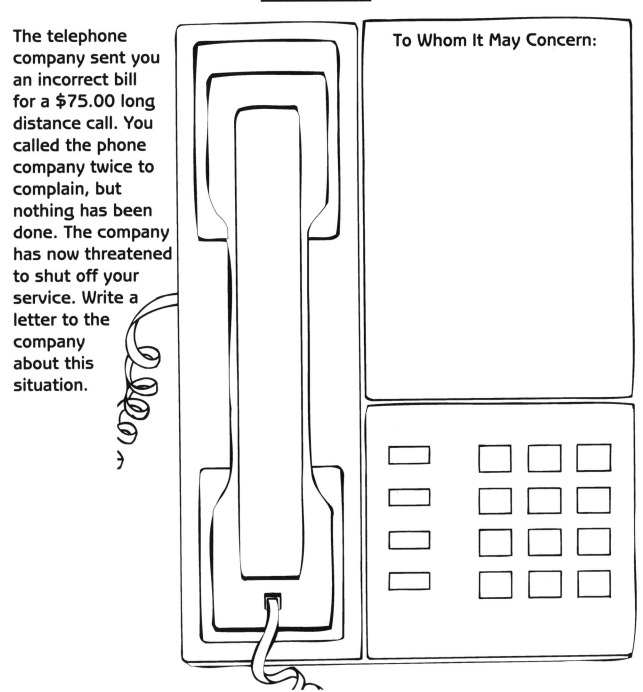

To Whom It May Concern:

Exercise 117:

An article has appeared in the newspaper naming you as the person who went on a rampage and smashed five car windows in a parking lot Write a letter to the paper demanding a *retraction*.

Exercise 118:

Your best friend has applied for a job as a grocery checker and has used you as a reference. Write a letter to the store's Personnel Office stating whether or not your friend would make a good employee and why this is the case.

Exercise 119:

You are forty-two years old and feeling a little depressed, so you decide to clean the attic of your house in order to take your mind off your troubles. You run across something in a shoe box that cheers you up. It is a letter from your grandmother. She wrote it to you when you were eight years old. What does the letter say?

Exercise 120:

You are a boy of thirteen at your first dance. Write the thoughts that run through your mind as you look across the room and see your best friend's sister sitting alone in a corner with a sad look on her face.

Exercise 121:

Finish this story: *Once upon a time in a land far away* there lived a troll whose ambition it was to move from his campsite under the bridge to a house near the river where he was sure he could live a better life.

Exercise 122:

Create a story that uses all of the following nouns. Use any other words that will connect the nouns into a whole piece.

rose	tooth	hands
washerwoman	mop	midnight
smiles	feet	tears

Exercise 123:

Write a _vignette_ about a _misanthrope_ who meets an _optimist_ on a train ride to St. Louis, Missouri.

_____

_____

_____

_____

_____

_____

_____

_____

_____

Exercise 124:

Write a page of dialogue between two people.
The subject of their conversation is *respect.*

Exercise 125:

Write a _monologue_ spoken by an old man who is sitting close to a camp-fire on a cold night in January.

Exercise 126:

Write a story called "*Missed Opportunity.*"
Use the following elements in it:

a train	*a clock*
Houston	*a nightmare*
Mr. Rodriguez	*rain*
a woman named Sally	*Mrs. Rodriguez*
a car	*a kind word*
an affliction	*a box of candy*
a red jacket	*a newspaper*
a diner	*a salt shaker*

Exercise 127:

Describe the difficulties that might develop in a relationship if one of the two parties had a problem with *lying*.

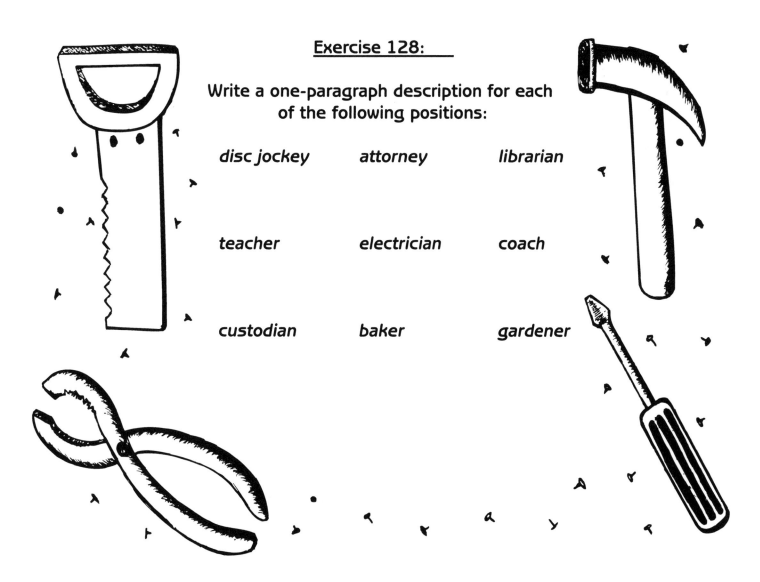

Exercise 128:

Write a one-paragraph description for each
of the following positions:

disc jockey   attorney   librarian

teacher   electrician   coach

custodian   baker   gardener

Exercise 129:

Write at least a paragraph about what each of these people have contri-
buted to society:

John Glenn   Chris Rock   Oprah Winfrey

Matthew Brady   Chief Joseph   Mark Twain

Exercise 130:

Make one *prepositional phrase* from each of the following prepositions:

Around

As

At

Beside

Beyond

By

For

From

In

Into

Of

Off

Out

Since

Through

To

Toward

With

Exercise 131:

Write ten sentences. Start five of them with <u>conjunctions</u>.
In the other five, use conjunctions to connect dependent or independent clauses, phrases, and words. <u>Underline</u> two of the strongest sentences. Why do you think so?

1. _____

2. _____

3. _____

4. _____

5. _____

1. _____

2. _____

3. _____

4. _____

5. _____

Kosovo

Write a one page report on the subject of <u>Kosovo</u>. Include a recount of events that occurred there in the past few years.

Exercise 133:

Write a one page summary about the lives of at least two of the following people:

Kofe Annan   *Theodore Roosevelt*   *Bill Clinton*

Leonardo da Vinci   *Bill Gates*

Exercise 134:

Who were these people? What made them famous?

Johnny Appleseed   *Marilyn Monroe*

Socrates   *Diogenes*

Exercise 135:

What was the *Emancipation Proclamation*? What part did it play in the history of slavery in the United States?

Exercise 136:

What are *percussion instruments*? How do they work? Name some.

Exercise 137:

Name four of William Shakespeare's plays.

Cite lines from the plays that are quoted to this day.

_____

_____

_____

_____

_____

_____

_____

Exercise 138:

Rewrite the following paragraph. You can extend it into more than one paragraph if you choose.

My heart goes out to ragamuffins, truants, people walking dogs, dogs themselves, the time it takes to fix an ATM thus making people late to work, the stinking highways that make everyone late, and, incidentally, the pool repair guy down the block who just went out of business.

Exercise 139:

If you are "*Livin' La Vida Loca*" what are you doing with your time? Describe your days in no less than one paragraph.

Exercise 140:

Explain the process you would use to teach a person to tell time. What would be the first step? And then?

Exercise 141:

List ten movie stars who made films during the 1930's and 1940's. Give examples of films each made.

1. _____

2. _____

3. _____

4. _____

5. _____

6. _____

7. _____

8. _____

9. _____

10. _____

Exercise 142:

Describe a person (other than your parents) whose kindness made your life happier when you were young.

Exercise 143:

Learn to spell the following words:

monologue   eccentric   troll   cafeteria   develop   stylish

Exercise 144:

What do each of the following expressions mean?

in the drink

shed some light

lose touch

Exercise 145:

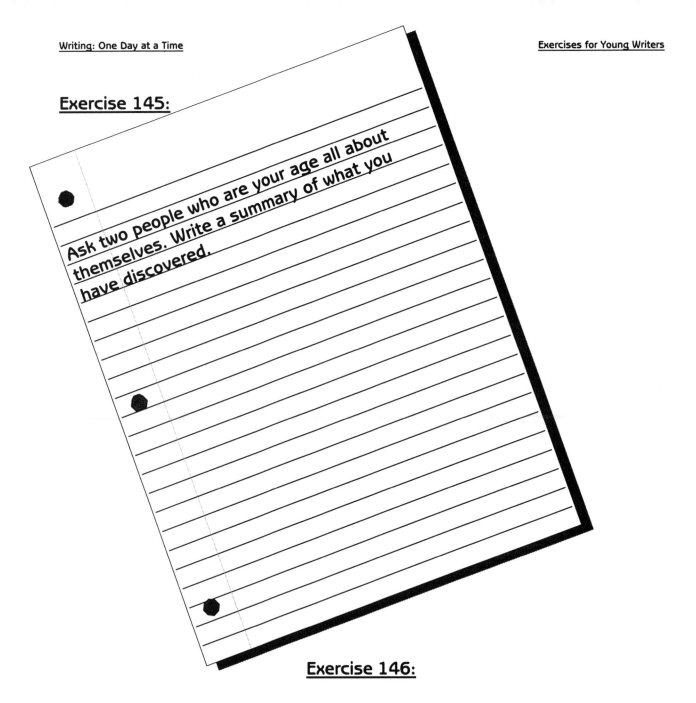

Ask two people who are your age all about themselves. Write a summary of what you have discovered.

Exercise 146:

Research the game of *Canasta*. Write a one page paper on the results of your investigation. Work from an outline you produce before you start your paper.

Exercise 147:

Write an autobiographical sketch that covers what you have been doing for the last two years.

Exercise 148:

Write an employment history of one of your parents.

YOUR OPINION, PLEASE

Write your opinion about the following topics in compositions no more than one page long.

Exercise 149:   How is *road rage* related to *respect*?

Exercise 150:   Why is *forgiveness* so difficult for most people?

Exercise 151:   What is *tolerance* and why is it important?

Exercise 152:   Why are *genuine* apologies difficult?

Exercise 153:   Explain love. How does it work?

Exercise 154:   Once a person is elected to public office, he or she often loses touch with the voters. True or False? Explain.

Exercise 155:   What is a "good education?"

Exercise 156:   Why are people interested in hearing about or watching court trials?

Exercise 157:   Some people say that you have to be strong in order to compromise. Is that true? Why?

Exercise 158:   How important is money?

Exercise 159:   What strengths or weaknesses might develop in a person who was raised in a one-parent home?

Exercise 160:   Is there ever a good reason to go to war?

Exercise 161:   Can the Physical Education classes that students take while they are in school help them in later life? In what ways?

Exercise 162:   What is the most exciting sport to watch? Why?

Exercise 163:   What is "woman's work?"

Exercise 164:   People talk about _civility_ as if it was something that used to exist in society, but no longer does. What do you think about it? Did people treat each other with more respect in the past? Do people treat each other badly these days?

Exercise 165:   Is there a type of person who is attracted to police work? How about military service? Are there people suited for that line of work who would have a hard time working elsewhere? Explain.

Exercise 166:   What does the term _economic development_ mean? What are the advantages of _economic development_? What are the disadvantages?

Exercise 167:   What is a _juvenile delinquent_? What characterizes the behavior of a person so named? When you hear the term _juvenile delinquent_, do you think about both boys and girls, or just boys? Why?

Exercise 168:   How do define the word _grace_? What does it mean when it is used to describe people with _athletic_ abilities? How about _artistic_ abilities? How about _Amazing Grace_? What does that mean?

LET'S GET PERSONAL - ONE-PAGERS

Exercise 169:   How would you handle a bully who made you his target?

Exercise 170:   Who was your first real friend outside your family? What was that person like?

Exercise 171:   What made your best Christmas a standout from all the rest?

Exercise 172:   What things about yourself would you like to improve?

Exercise 173:   How did your family's financial situation affect your early upbringing?

Exercise 174:   What was your first understanding of how law enforcement works in the community?

Exercise 175:   When was your first realization of personal limitations?

Exercise 176:   What was your first persistent worry? How did you cope with it? Did you have help from anyone?

Exercise 177:   What caused your first reaction to insects? How about snakes?

Exercise 178: Where were you in the *birth order* of your family? Did it make a difference in your upbringing? Explain.

_____

_____

_____

_____

_____

Exercise 179: What is the <u>age</u> <u>of</u> <u>majority</u>? Have you reached it? Have others you know reached it? What happens to some people when they reach it?

Exercise 180: How many different items of clothing do you have? Make an inventory. Include shoes and boots.

Exercise 181:

Using no more than seven sentences, describe what your actions or feelings would be if you walked in the bathroom and behind the shower curtain someone was taking a shower. Use dialogue if you want.

_____

_____

_____

Exercise 182:

Write two paragraphs. In the first, describe what your ambition was when you were six years old. In the second, write what it is now.

then

now

Exercise 183:

Write at least five synonyms for each of the following words:

neat

wonderful _____ _____ _____ _____ _____

stupid _____ _____ _____ _____ _____

sweet _____ _____ _____ _____ _____

sad					

terrible _____

Exercise 184:

Learn to spell these words:

acquaint　　　　imbecile　　　　moody

degradable　　　lamprey　　　　piquant

ilk　　　　　　　laudable　　　　saturnine

Exercise 185:

How do you play the game of *Ping Pong*? What are its rules?
What equipment is needed?

Exercise 186:

Write at least two paragraphs that give advice to a person who believes most people do not like him. Use a letter format if you wish.

Exercise 187:

Make a *times table* for seven numbers of your choice.
Start each table with 1 times (x) your number, and end it with 12 times (x) your number.

1						
2						
3						
4						
5						
6						
7						
8						
9						
10						
11						
12						

Exercise 188:

List the names of as many children as you can who were in your third grade class.

Exercise 189:

Make a list of 30 countries in the world.
Include at least two countries from each continent.

1.   16.

2.   17.

3.   18.

4.   19.

5.   20.

6.   21.

7.   22.

8.   23.

9.   24.

0.   25.

11.   26.

12.   27.

13.   28.

14.   29.

15.   30.

Exercise 190:

In no less than one page, write about how hatred can develop in a person.

Exercise 191:

List in each section of the soccer ball the kind of pressures that might develop among the players of a soccer team. Explain.

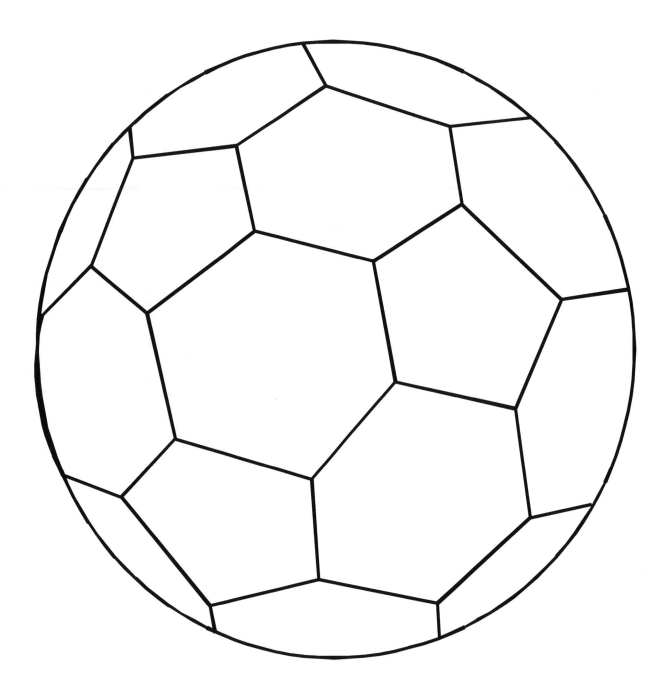

Exercise 192:

In ancient times, a newborn child was sometimes left on a hillside to die if it looked weak or deformed at birth. What do you think of this practice? Write at least one page explaining your answer.

Exercise 193:

What are your feelings about a man who, during a time of war, declares himself to be a *conscientious objector*? Write your ideas in the plaque.

Exercise 194:

How important is privacy? Explain your answer. Use examples from your own life.

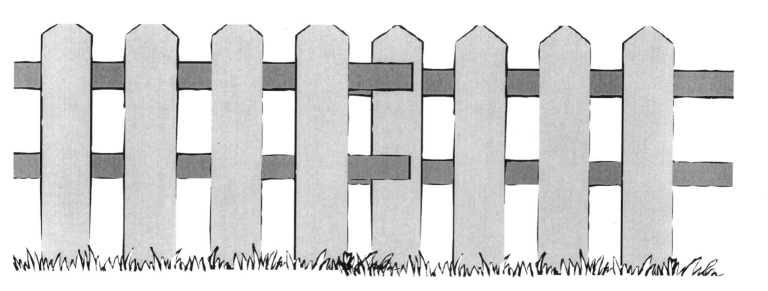

Exercise 195:

What are the characteristics of an emotionally healthy personality?

Exercise 196:

You are a foreman on a construction job. A worker in your crew named Jacob Smith has been injured and taken to a hospital. Fill out an accident report form describing the circumstances. The sections of the report are these:

Name of Injured _____

Date and Time of Injury _____

Cause of Injury _____

The report also calls for a description of the action you took at the time of the injury, and your opinion about how such an injury could be prevented in the future.

_____

_____

_____

_____

_____

_____

_____

Exercise 197:

How do *workaholics* behave? Give examples.

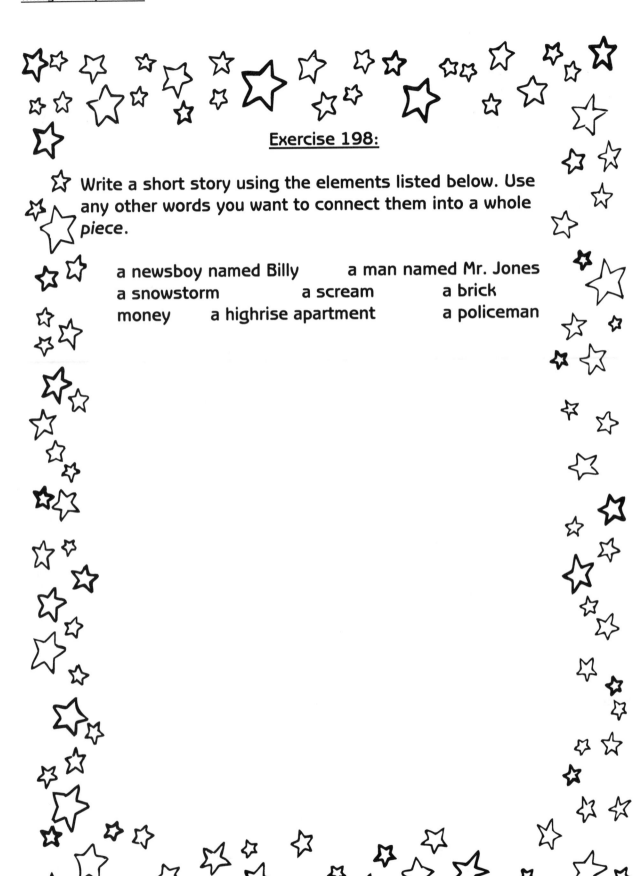

Exercise 198:

Write a short story using the elements listed below. Use any other words you want to connect them into a whole piece.

a newsboy named Billy   a man named Mr. Jones
a snowstorm   a scream   a brick
money   a highrise apartment   a policeman

Exercise 199:

What do these words mean?
Write two sentences. Use two of the words in each sentence, making sure you use all 3 words within the two sentences.

emphasize _____

impatient _____

vaudeville _____

1.

2.

3.

Exercise 200:

Choose five more letters in the alphabet. For each letter you choose, write a sentence in which every word begins with that letter. For example, if you choose the letter "b" your sentence might read:

Buster bought bagels.

The LAST PAGE

If you have reached this point by completing as many of the Exercises as you could, let me offer my sincere congratulations for a job well done. Your self confidence has no doubt increased because of your *feat*.

You have a right to feel very good about yourself. Doing things that are difficult makes success even sweeter, so take a bow. You deserve it.

On the other hand, if you have not done many of the Exercises and are just checking out the page for whatever information you can *glean* from it, I bid you greetings.

The journey on the way to a *personal best* does, after all, begin with one step.

By the way, I am known as *Miss Bass*.

Exercise 201:

What's your name?

_____

Appendix for <u>Writing: one day at a time</u>

The purpose of the following pages is to support your students as they journey through the Exercises. They include ideas about

Imagination and Context

Making Lists (brainstorming)

Details

Components of a Well Written Paragraph

Grammatical Reminders

The following pages can be 1) transferred into transparencies and discussed with the appropriate exercises; 2) duplicated as handouts and distributed as topics arise; and 3) developed into motivational or reference bulletin boards as applicable exercises occur.

Included in <u>Writing: one day at a time</u> are prompts (exercises) for narratives (stories with details, a beginning, middle and end); expository writing (instructional, informational explanation with examples); persuasive writing (persuasion with examples and details) and descriptive writing.
If you prepare for state writing assessments, you may want students to create a bulletin board with the headings of Narrative, Expository, Persuasive, Descriptive. Then, as Exercises are completed, samples can be placed under the appropriate category.

The sample borders can be used as "story borders" that students can use for writing exercises.

Imagination and Context

Pay attention to things you don't understand.

When you think about such things, imagine

you can hold them in the palm of your hand.

Imagine that you can turn them to the left and

then to the right. Imagine that you can turn

them upside down and inside out.

If you make use of your imagination in such a way,

an edge of some knowledge about those

mysterious things will very likely emerge.

Context is an important idea, but people

don't pay much attention to it.

Context can determine the meaning of words,

so it can make a big difference

in how your writing is understood by others.

Lists

1. Lists are wonderful tools for accomplishing goals.

2. List-making helps you feel in control of your business.

3. List-making creates a feeling of well-being.

4. Lists are useful in the process of getting organized.

5. Lists sometimes inspire a vision of the future.

6. Lists can also help you reconstruct the past.

LET'S HEAR IT FOR LISTS!

Details

Suppose you wanted to let someone know how to bake a cake.

You could use a format such as a recipe, or you could use a more free-flowing <u>narrative</u> style to describe the process. In either case, the effectiveness of the description would rest upon your use of <u>details</u>.

Details are the building blocks of good writing. Readers enjoy putting details together so they can understand all parts of a writer's vision. Details are the clues a reader follows, so you want them clear. If they are not, you will lose the reader. That's not what you want to happen.

<u>Descriptive</u> writing has certain satisfactions, not the least of which is exercising the power to discard. Discard what? Extraneous information and details! The trick is to decide just what is extraneous.

Read the dictionary any chance you get. To write well, you need to feel at home in the company of words.

That's where editing comes in. Don't get too attached to your own words. Edit and move on!

A Well Written Paragraph

starts with

a **topic sentence** and does not stray

too far from the basic idea of the

sentence. The paragraph that

follows the topic sentence

explains the idea in the

sentence, or at least sheds some

light on it.

Not only do good paragraphs contain strong topic sentences,

but they also have

snappy, on-target **conclusions**.

**Good conclusions are the bridges
that readers can cross
as they follow your line of thinking.**

GRAMMATICAL REMINDERS

1. Use commas to separate items in a series.

   Example: *The American flag is red, white, and blue.*

2. <u>Don't</u> use commas to separate a subject and predicate.

   Example: *He, jumped.*

3. Use commas to separate adjectives that modify the same noun.

   Example: *She was a sweet, wonderful sister.*

4. Use quotation marks when you quote someone.

   Example: *Mary said, "I am going to be an important writer someday."*

5. Use quotation marks when you want to redefine a word for a special purpose.

   Example: *The information was not current. It was "stale" news.*

6. Separate two independent clauses in a sentence by a comma placed before the connecting conjunction.

   Example: *I went to the store, and I bought milk.*

7. Separate two independent clauses in a sentence with a semi-colon if there is no connecting conjunction.

   Example: *I went to the store; I wanted to buy milk.*

ABOUT COMMAS

Of all the problems writers face, none can produce more anxiety than trying to get the commas right.

Commas exist to clear things up, not obfuscate them. Using too many commas in a piece of writing is like putting too much salt in the stew.

Better to under-use commas than to fall headlong "into the drink" from one comma too many.

ABOUT APOSTROPHES

Trying to use apostrophes correctly can also elevate your heart beat. Writers are often confused about where to place them.

Some writers use them indiscriminately and hope for the best, while others leave them out entirely.

There is a middle ground!

The job of an apostrophe is to show possession before adding an "s" to a noun.

Another way to use apostrophes is in forming contractions. If you've used them in plurals, you've missed the boat.

There is no such thing as "I put the <u>package's</u> in my room."

ABOUT CONJUNCTIONS

Conjunctions are great little organizers.

They keep us from slipping into gibberish by neatly separating our ideas.

Conjunctions! Stand up and take a bow!

and or but for neither either nor

ABOUT PREPOSITIONS

Prepositional phrases give readers details.

"Meet me <u>by the fountain</u>," he said, "<u>around a quarter to ten</u>."

Precise! Intriguing!

ON CONTEXT

Critics will sometimes say this to writers: "Look here, you can't mix apples and oranges!"

Actually, you can mix apples and oranges if you establish a <u>context</u> in which they can co-exist. For example, if you write about picnics or banquets, you can create a context in which it is perfectly all right to mix apples and oranges.

Context is a mysterious thing. Work hard at learning its secrets.

Use your imagination and complete this story border.

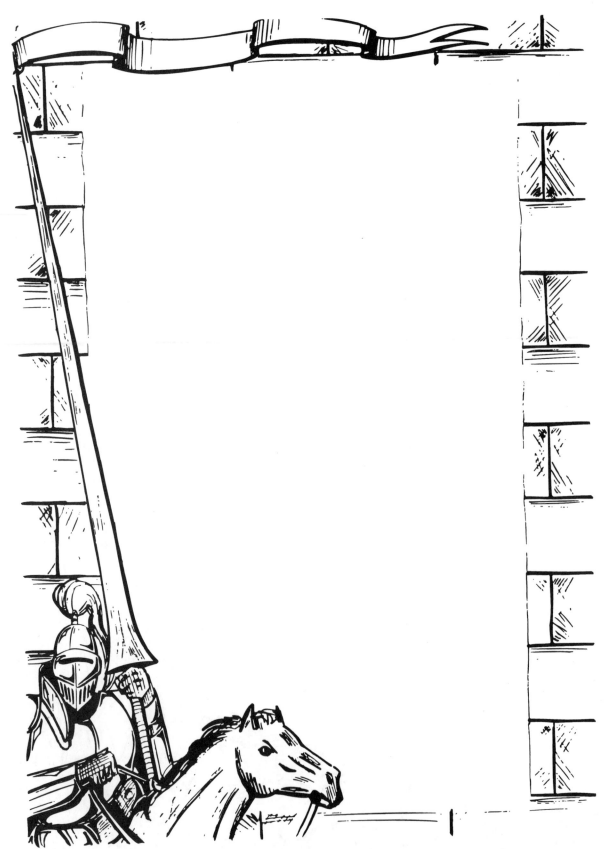

Use your imagination and complete this story border.